D0700957

1. A totally destroyed Pz Kpfw IV Ausf H rests in a field near Vaucelles, France, 18 July 1944, its high-velocity 7.5cm still defiantly spiking the sky. (PA–114368/Public Archives of Canada)

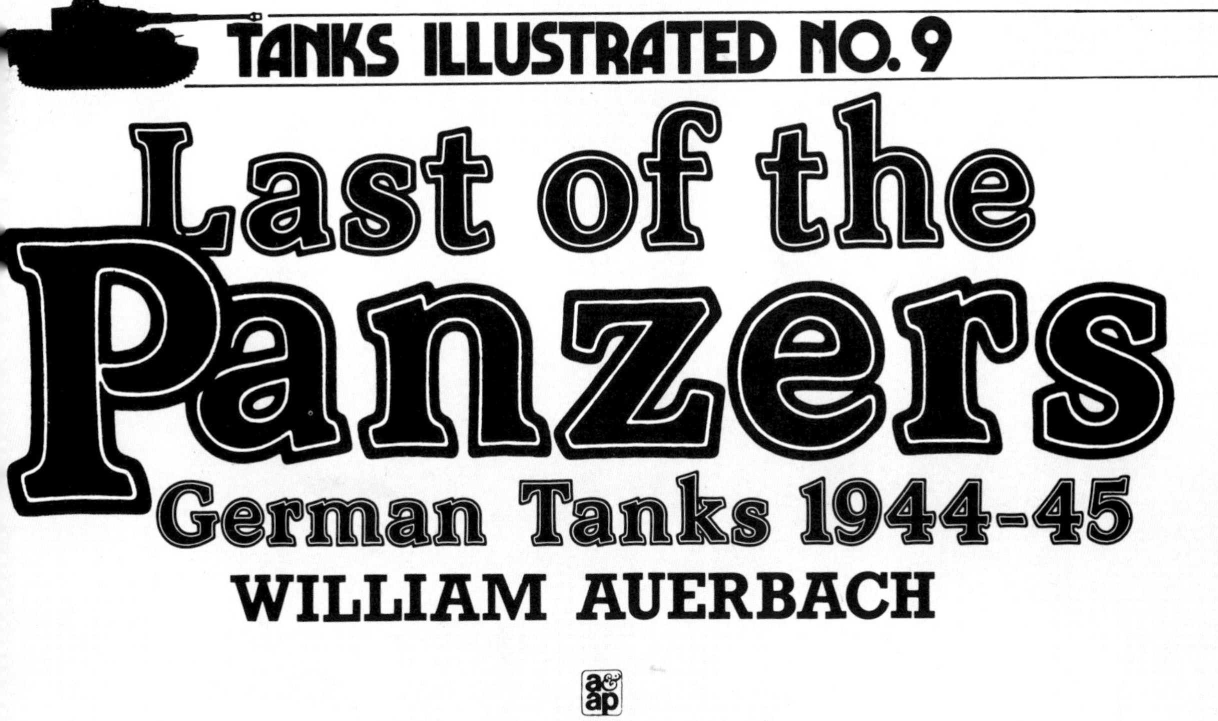

TANKS ILLUSTRATED NO. 9

Last of the Panzers

German Tanks 1944–45

WILLIAM AUERBACH

a&ap

ARMS AND ARMOUR PRESS

London – Melbourne – Harrisburg, Pa. – Cape Town

Introduction

Tanks Illustrated 9: Last of the Panzers
Published in 1984 by
Arms and Armour Press, Lionel Leventhal Limited, 2–6 Hampstead High Street, London NW3 1QQ; 4–12 Tattersalls Lane, Melbourne, Victoria 3000, Australia; Sanso Centre, 8 Adderley Street, P.O. Box 94, Cape Town 8000; Cameron and Kelker Streets, P.O. Box 1831, Harrisburg, Pennsylvania 17105, USA

British Library Cataloguing in Publication Data:
Auerbach, William
Last of the Panzers. – (Tanks illustrated; 9)
1. Germany. *Heer* – History – Pictorial works
2. Tanks (Military science) – History – Pictorial works
I. Title II. Series
623.74′752′0943 UG446.5
ISBN 0–85368–632–7

Edited by Michael Boxall.
Layout by Roger Chesneau.
Printed and bound in Great Britain by William Clowes Limited, Beccles and London.

2. A 'Nashorn'/'Hornisse' knocked out in a duel with an M10 tank destroyer of the French First Army on the Colmar Plain, Riedwihr area of France, 7 February 1945. Otherwise known as the 8.8cm PaK43/1(L/71) auf Fahrgestell Pz Kpfw III/IV(Sf), its travel lock could be disengaged by a cable running down from the crossbar to a pipe-like conduit which snakes along the driver's extended cab. The tracks are fitted with chevrons and ice grips.

The brute force and tactical proficiency of Hitler's Panzer Armies were intrinsically linked to Germany's production facilities and supplies of raw materials; once stripped of its air cover and over-extended in Russia, the ensuing war of attrition was not one the Germans, fighting on two fronts, could win. This is a straightforward pictorial account of the dissolution of the vaunted Panzer divisions during the last year of the war in Italy and Northwest Europe, and depicts a broad cross-section of late-production types, seldom seen in one volume. Certainly no other combatant fielded such a variety of vehicles as did the Germans; the Teutonic preference for carefully crafted machines collided enough times with the demands for mass production and redesign to ensure students of armour an intriguing array of AFVs to study for years to come, and I hope the photographs selected for this book give the reader a better understanding of German armour of the period.

Special care has been taken to provide accurate, informative captions, and I have attempted to highlight those factors that need to be considered as a whole when identifying certain models. Dates and locations, however, were taken verbatim from the original captions and were based solely upon the photographers' knowledge at the time. This being the case, discretion is advised before accepting any date or place as absolute.

While assembling the pictures for this book I asked myself why German armour has long held its fascination for those of us predisposed to such things in the first place. I believe it is because they looked the part: capable, efficient and, above all, lethal. One can imagine the Panther, with its sloping armour and vaulting drive sprockets, ranging over the battlefield, stiff-arming its opponents with its long-barrelled '75' until the odds against them simply became overwhelming. While the assortment was impressive and the technology enviable, the numbers tell the story. Every vehicle you see here was lost to Germany at a time when it could least afford it, and, many times, a highly skilled crew was lost as well.

The photographs are arranged chronologically where possible, and unless otherwise noted all are US Army Photographs from the Signal Corps collection. My thanks to Bill Miley, who generously contributed photographs from Colonel G.B. Jarrett's collection at Carlisle Barracks, and to Dan Graves, who helped immensely by printing many of the photographs shown. I am especially indebted to Tom Jentz, Technical Editor of *Encyclopedia of German Tanks*, for his considerable help in identifying those models of the Pz Kpfw III and IV whose exact designations were predicated upon subtle design changes, and for providing insight and encouragement throughout this project.

William Auerbach, 1984

▲3 ▼4

3. American infantrymen of the 133rd Regiment, 34th Division, US Fifth Army, passing a Jagdpanzer 38(t) Hetzer on Highway 9, Modena, Italy, 23 April 1945. The mantlet, roughly finished and decorated with two 'eyes', identifies the vehicle as a late model. The sloping lower hull sides are very evident, as is the large amount of foliage draped on the vehicle for added camouflage. The auxiliary remote-controlled MG42 sights have been removed by its crew.

4. Canadian troops examine a StuG III Ausf G near Pignatora, Italy, 6 May 1944. The shield for the loader's MG is to the right of the soldier on top of the vehicle. (PA–130350/Public Archives of Canada)

5. The heavy fighting which took place near Pontecorvo, Italy, is reflected in the devastation surrounding this StuG IV knocked out by the 48th Highlanders, 19 May 1944. The concrete reinforcement on the driver's cab is cracked, and additional armour plate appears to have been fitted to the side of the cab. Note the hinged sun visors on the driver's periscopes and the additional armour bolted to the right front superstructure which may also have been covered with concrete. (PA–130353/Public Archives of Canada)

6. In the Castelonorato area of Italy, 16 May 1944, troops of the Anti-Tank Company, 85th Division bring in a captured Panzerjäger 38(t), giving an idea of the small size of this vehicle. This Marder III has the rounded, cast cover for the driver's compartment and only one return roller.

7. This Sturmgeschütz IV had its StuK40 L/48 blown right out of it, along with the superstructure roof, by British Churchill tanks working with the Canadians in Pontecorvo, Italy, 24 May 1944. The driver's extended compartment with periscopes fitted is shown to good advantage, and has a cross on its side. This StuG IV, bearing diagonally-patterned zimmerit, has four steel return rollers and carries spare bogies like the Pz Kpfw IV. All that is left of the steel-plate schurzen is the angle-iron bracket. (PA–130340/Public Archives of Canada)

5▲

6▲ 7▼

8. Another victim of Canadian armour in the Pontecorvo area of Italy, photographed 25 May 1944 as soldiers inspect the damage. Note how the zimmerit was applied only to those areas not covered by the schurzen. This is a Pz Kpfw IV Ausf H with basic 80mm frontal armour interlocked, and no side vision ports for the driver or radio operator. (PA–130355/Public Archives of Canada)

9. Nice view of a Panther Ausf A with the letter-box flap MG port instead of the more familiar ball mount. The Ausf A designation depended more on changes to the turret than anything else. Note the new cupola, loader's episcope and absence of a pistol port in the turret side. This Panther was knocked out in the Liri Valley, Italy, and photographed on 25 May 1944. (PA–130354/Public Archives of Canada)

10. The 5th Canadian Armored Brigade was credited with this 'Nashorn' knocked out by a PIAT near Pontecorvo, Italy. The gun is still secured in its travel lock, indicating that the crew was caught by surprise. Unusual is the fact that the rear tow hooks are missing from both sides. Note the number '2' painted on the rear plate. The photograph was taken on 26 May 1944. (PA–130348/ Public Archives of Canada)

11. American and Allied troops clamber over this Panther Ausf A in the San Giovanni area of Italy, 26 May 1944. The raked rear hull is fitted with a tow shackle and there are additional stowage lockers on each side of the engine deck, indicating that the troops thought it prudent to be able to tow or carry supplies even if it meant sacrificing some of the fighting capability of their vehicle.

▲8 ▼9

10▲ 11▼

▲12 ▼13

12. A Pz Kpfw IV Ausf H, no. 725, abandoned in a haystack near Sezze, Italy, 29 May 1944. This one carries extra 30mm armour bolted to the superstructure front. Zimmerit on the Ausf H was applied in the field instead of at the factory. Note the glass blocks in the driver's side visor and the one-piece cupola hatch.
13. Members of a Canadian light AA regiment look over a 'Nashorn' near Pontecorvo, Italy, 30 May 1944. The armour on the fighting compartment has been blown away revealing the mount for the 8.8cm PaK43/1. Note the plate behind the idler that pushed loose track pins back into position. (PA–130346/Public Archives of Canada)
14. The suspension of this Panther Ausf G tells the story here. A hollow charge round struck the turret side and everything inside, including the torsion bars, was blown out. Note the plug for the bow MG, and factory-applied zimmerit. 20 June 1944, near Bretteville, France. (PA–130149/Public Archives of Canada)
15. RCA troops pick through the remains of a Pz Kpfw IV Ausf H near Pontecorvo, Italy, 26 May 1944. Note how the turret armour protected the turret ring. (PA-130341/Public Archives of Canada)
16. A leading Sturmgeschütz IV of a panzer spearhead which came under rocket attack and retreated into a field where it was set on fire. The vehicle's armour was completely ruptured by the resulting explosions. Note the late-pattern sprocket, steel return rollers and 30mm plate bolted to the right side of the superstructure front. (US Air Force Photograph)

14▲

15▲ 16▼

17. This burned-out Panther Ausf A was found blocking a road near Marigny-Montrevil, France, the day after being attacked by rocket-firing aircraft. A Pz Kpfw IV Ausf H or J mired itself trying to go round it. (US Air Force Photograph)
18. GIs of the 133rd Infantry Division examine a Tiger I Ausf E, stopped by a 75mm round in the flank, during a counterattack in the Cecina area of Italy, 3 July 1944. This late-production model, with the new cupola and resilient steel wheels, has a thick layer of zimmerit on the turret, of a different pattern from that on the rest of the vehicle.
19. Sturmgeschütz IV caught in the bocage by rocket-firing aircraft and put out of action near Marigny-Montrevil, France. The hatches over the driver's cab and commander's cupola are open. The vehicle has zimmerit, and a spare track on the hull front and driver's compartment. (US Air Force Photograph)

▲17 ▼18

19▼

20. In the Canadian sector a 'Wespe' turns up, disabled with its howitzer jammed in full recoil. The redesigned air louvres of this SP fit right into the sides of the superstructure, giving the vehicle very clean lines. German crosses are carried on both sections of the shield. The tracks, unusually, are installed backwards. (Author's collection)

21. A rare Pz Kpfw II Ausf L 'Luchs' reconnaissance vehicle, which looks very like a miniature Tiger I. The vehicle's lack of interior space has necessitated the carriage of numerous storage boxes outside, leaving little room there either. The turret number '4134' has been painted right across the clutter. (Author's collection)

▲20 ▼21

22▲

22. One of fifty-four 15cm sFH13/1(Sf) auf GW Lorraine Schlepper (f)s still available to the Germans in 1944, appears in dazzling splinter camouflage in the Canadian sector soon after the invasion. The recoil spade is in the raised position and the vehicle number is obscured by foliage draped over its side. (Author's collection)

23. Front view of the same vehicle showing the driver's compartment wide open. The travel lock is folded down directly behind the visored flap. (Author's collection)

24. Rear view showing the lengthened recoil spade and access door. Note the chain used to raise and lower the spade, and the symbol indicating a fully-tracked artillery vehicle. (Author's collection)

◀23

24▼

▲25

25. A thoroughly crippled Pz Kpfw IV Ausf G litters the Agira-Regalbuto road near Pachino Beach, Sicily, 3 July 1944. Its distinguishing features are the side vision port for the driver and the smoke dischargers on the turret front. The conical pistol port, which is normally overshadowed by the rear stowage bin, is plainly visible in this photograph. (PA–130337/Public Archives of Canada)

26. A US jeep passes a pair of Pz Kpfw IVs on the road to Pontedera, Italy, 18 July 1944. The first vehicle, an Ausf J, has no auxiliary engine muffler, but has the 'H' muzzle brake and zimmerit. The rear vehicle is an Ausf H with brackets for air filters and antenna rods on the hull sides. The number '834' has been painted over field-applied zimmerit. It also has the late sprocket/early idler and one-piece hatch. Both panzers have four steel return rollers.

27. A US soldier peers down the hatch of the driver's extended box on a Sturmgeschütz IV in Periers, France, 24 July 1944. Called 'Scharnhorst' by its crew, it has the late sprocket/idler, steel return rollers, zimmerit, schurzen and additional 30mm plate bolted on the right superstructure front. Its jack is propped against the drive sprocket.

28. A rather dishevelled FlaKpanzer 38(t) and the possibility of snipers are all that threaten US troops in Torigni-sur-Vire, France, 3 August 1944. The vehicle has the early cast cover for the driver's compartment bolted on the glacis. A shop sign in the background appears to be part of the 2cm FlaK38 mount.

▼26

27▲ 28▼

▲29 ▼30

29. A patrol from the 35th Infantry Division follows up an American artillery barrage into Pontfaroy, France, 3 August 1944, passing a Pz Kpfw IV Ausf H amid the ruins. The vehicle's right track is broken and dust obscures the German cross and stencilled outlines of the number '802' on the turret schurzen. The hull armour is interlocked, the driver's side visor is absent and the muzzle brake is of the late, round pattern. Note the early sprocket/idler in combination with four steel return rollers.
30. The same vehicle photographed two days later from a different angle shows the pistol ports in the turret doors and the 'Nahverteidigungswaffe' on the turret roof, but no lugs for the 2-ton crane. The 2nd Panzer Division's trident insignia appears on the left front superstructure corner.
31. The wide tracks of this Panther Ausf A ploughed up mounds of earth before grinding to a halt in the face of the American advance on St Pois, France, 5 August 1944. Notice the 'letter-box' flap for the driver, and the plug for the bow MG mount. (The inner sleeve of the MG protrudes from the barrel.) (US Army Official Photograph)
32. Front ¾ view of a StuG III Ausf G, its welded mantlet covered with chicken wire to hold foliage for camouflage. This vehicle is almost factory fresh, and carries full schurzen plates with the number '212' and a thick German cross painted on them. The loader has the hinged shield for use with his MG in either the AA or ground role. (Author's collection)
33. French vehicles which had been pressed into German service are lined up at a collection-point somewhere in France, 7 August 1944. The first is a Munitionsschlepper 35R, followed by a Pz Kpfw 38H 735(f) with the 3.7cm KwK38(f) L/33 and the same vehicle with the short 3.7cm KwK18(f) L/21. Note the split hatches on the turrets replacing the original cupola.

31▲

32▲ 33▼

◀34 ▲35

34. Front view of a Jagdpanzer IV. The series went from 60mm superstructure to an 80mm one. This one still has the 60mm plate, but the MG port on the left side has been welded shut, in anticipation of its complete deletion later on when the longer gun was introduced. Note the zimmerit and the threads for the discontinued muzzle brake. (Author's collection)

35. Front view of a StuG III Ausf G built on a converted Pz Kpfw III Ausf J chassis, distinguishable by the hull roof hatch (in raised position in front of driver). This vehicle was probably produced in May 1943, and carries a thick application of concrete on the superstructure front and sides. The channel iron on the bow secured extra track links when they were carried.

36. This 'Wespe' was destroyed by American troops at Mortree, France, 16 August 1944. Mounting the 10.5cm light field howitzer in a modified Pz Kpfw II chassis, it was a more economical SP than the American 'Priest'. The driver's compartment is shown completely opened up, and the SP artillery tactical symbol is just visible in front of the sprocket.

▼36

37▲ 38▼

7. A Sturmpanzer IV from the last production series is gone over ɔr booby-traps after being abandoned. This 'Brummbär' is fitted ʼith the auxiliary MG in the front superstructure and the box for ɪe driver, giving only periscopic vision. Track links dot the heavy ɔating of zimmerit. (Author's collection)

38. GIs look over a Panther Ausf A which appears to have been holed through its glacis, an extremely difficult thing to do at any range. The main gun was probably tracking a flanking vehicle when a tank destroyer or 'Firefly' drilled it. Note the troop-applied zimmerit. (Author's collection)

39. Front $\frac{3}{4}$ view of a Pz Kpfw IV Ausf H with interlocked 80mm basic hull armour, Elboeuf, France, 27 August 1944. Although fitted with steel return rollers, it retains the early-pattern idler. All the schurzen plates, including those on the turret, have been lost, making it possible to see that the driver's side visor has been deleted, but that the pistol ports in the turret doors are still fitted. Note that zimmerit anti-magnetic paste has been applied in only a few places. (PA–130188/Public Archives of Canada)

40. Local farmworkers study a Pz Kpfw IV Ausf H which has tried to make do with a damaged track, by looping the shortened track from the return roller directly to the first road wheel. Note the steel return rollers, the absence of a driver's side visor, and the vision device in the turret door. The turret schurzen was surprisingly rigid and usually stayed on long after the side plates were lost. Villy, France, 26 August 1944. (PA–130181/Public Archives of Canada)

41. A Canadian 'Staghound' with bridging sections passes a burned out Tiger II and a Bergepanther on the side of the road. The Tiger II is interesting because it has the early-production Porsche turret, zimmerit and the late-production drive sprocket with redesigned track. It also carries a ladder on its hull side. The Bergepanther lacks a winch, but has the extended exhaust pipes, angled outwards here. (PA–39049/Public Archives of Canada)

▼39

40▲ 41▼

▲42

42. A Canadian soldier measures the battle track of a steel-wheeled Tiger I Ausf E which took considerable punishment before being destroyed in Tosters, France, 30 August 1944. The tank sustained at least a dozen hits before being penetrated above the driver's visor, and a partial penetration is visible under its barrel. The engine hatch is open and the bow machine-gun has been removed indicating that the vehicle may have been abandoned. The number '223' appears on the turret side over troop-applied zimmerit. (PA–114159/Public Archives of Canada)

43. A front ¾ view of a Marder II, abandoned in its concealed position, somewhere in France. The rounded muzzle brake on the PaK40/2 suggests that the vehicle is one of the seventy-five Marder IIs converted just prior to March 1944. Its travel lock lies against the hull and there is a large stowage locker on the right front trackguard. (Author's collection)

44. Captured in the Canadian sector, an Artillerie-Panzerbeobachtungswagen based on the Pz Kpfw III Ausf G. Note the dummy barrel with the MG in the centre of the thickened mantlet, the early cupola with split hatch, schurzen, factory zimmerit, extra bolt-on armour on the hull front and the unevenly-spaced return rollers. (Author's collection)

45. On their way to the River Arno, 1 September 1944, troops of the 92nd Division pass a late-production Tiger I Ausf E in the outskirts of Ponsacco. The vehicle has the periscope-equipped commander's cupola and resilient steel wheels. The turret stowage bin attachment points and escape hatch locking mechanism are clearly visible.

▼43

44▲ 45▼

▲46 ▼47

46. Captured vehicles parked in Isigny, France, 3 September 1944. Among the Panthers, Pz Kpfw IVs, StuG IIIs and Sd Kfz 251s are two of the diminutive Munitionsschlepper UE(f)s fitted with Wurfrahmen 40 frames. (US Army Official Photograph)
47. This derelict Pz Kpfw IV Ausf H sits with other wrecked German equipment in a field five miles west of Sees, France, 3 September 1944. The spare track wrapped around the corners of the superstructure indicates that the vision ports for driver and radio operator had been deleted.
48. The Germans made extensive use of captured French AFVs, up-rating their armament during remanufacture. Here are two examples sharing a depot with three Panther Ausf As, two miles south of Trevieres, France. The first is a 4.7cm PaK(t) auf Pz Kpfw 35R reconverted to an Artillerie Schlepper. The second is a 7.5cm PaK40/1 auf GW Lorraine Schlepper, named 'Löwe', with a stowage box fitted to its right hull side.

48▼

49. A StuG III Ausf F/8 Headquarters vehicle, no. 001 of 11th Panzer Division (note insignia on hull front), with a one-piece hatch over the transmission instead of the usual split and hinged type, photographed in the 45th Division's area in the southern part of Baume Les Dames, France, 12 September 1944. One hatch is jammed beside the mantlet, and the hull has been reinforced with additional armour plates.

50. The shambles a few tanks could make of a town, in this case, Meximieux, France, 4 September 1944. This Panther Ausf A, one of nine tanks knocked out by American armour, has chosen a bad spot in which to catch fire.

51. Front ¾ view of a 7.5cm PaK40/1 auf GW Lorraine Schlepper (f), no. 322, abandoned in Vesoul, France, 13 September 1944. Spare bogies are carried behind the travel lock, and the driver's open compartment is littered with a bazooka, rockets and 2cm ammunition. Note the handles and the 'tac' sign on the transmission housing and the bolted shield for the PaK40.

▲49 ▼50

2. A 3.7cm FlaK auf Fahrgestell Pz Kpfw IV (Sf) Möbelwagen') destroyed by the retreating ermans, Xertigny, France, 21 September 1944. ased on a Pz Kpfw IV Ausf J hull, it lacks the uffler for the auxiliary engine and vertical brackets n lower rear hull, but retains the early idler with te sprocket and four steel return rollers. Next to e bracket for the spare bogie is the radio aerial hich has been repositioned at an angle away from e vehicle. Note the circular pistol ports in slab ields and the gun cleaning rod at the rear. The top dge of the side shields is vertical; the other edges, hich are angled in, once extended beyond the front nd rear walls.

3. Another 3.7cm-equipped 'Möbelwagen', no. 11, based on the late Pz Kpfw IV Ausf J chassis, ith vertical exhaust mufflers, four steel return ollers and late sprocket/early idler combination. he side shields, again, are completely flat, but lack e two support brackets in this instance. The inged sections on the rear shield have been swung utwards.

51▲

52▲ 53▼

▲54 ▼55

56▲

54. Mid-production StuG III Ausf G, run aground near Luneville, France, 29 September 1944, sporting 30mm armour bolted to basic 50mm superstructure armour, steel return rollers, 'Saukopf', late-pattern muzzle brake, plated over opening for remote-controlled MG, 'Nahverteidigungswaffe', schurzen, lugs on roof for 2-ton crane, travel lock and zimmerit.
55. An infantryman of the 101st Airborne Division walks past a Panzerbefehlswagen V, lately the victim of a bazooka in fierce fighting near the village of Erp, Holland, 23 September 1944. The zimmerit has flaked off the turret where the rocket hit. The star aerial and the additional rod aerial betray its identity as a commander's vehicle.
56. Side view of a Panther Ausf G showing its stark outlines and 'chin' mantlet with rain guard. The side armour was increased on the upper hull side from 40mm to 50mm, and spare track was hung on the turret sides to increase protection. Note the total absence of zimmerit. (C–84047/Public Archives of Canada)
57. Front ¾ view of 'Sofi', a very successful Panzerjäger 38(t) with upwards of 30 kills to its credit. This model of the Marder III has the welded cover for the driver's compartment, sporting a cartoon-like drawing of a bird, and the hull sides extended to form towing brackets. A small cross appears on the right hull front. Next to the Marder is a maintenance/munitions vehicle on a Pz Kpfw III chassis. (PA–52084/Public Archives of Canada)

57▼

58. Standing out against the flat terrain of Ploy, France, is this knocked out Panther Ausf G, 14 October 1944. The zimmerit was applied by the troops and has a very coarse pattern. The number '252' is painted on the turret and the cupola is fitted with the AA MG mount.

252

▲59 ▼60

61▲

59. Although a poor photograph, this picture is included because it shows a StuH42 with a coaxial MG in the mantlet and waffle-pattern zimmerit. Note the rifling in the barrel, which is not fitted with a muzzle brake. Woendrecht, Holland, 1 November 1944. (PA–130332/Public Archives of Canada)
60. Fine view of a Hetzer wearing a textbook application of the late 'ambush' paint scheme. The three primary colours of red-brown, dark green and sand were applied and then the lighter colours were dappled over the darker colours and vice versa, producing a sunlight-through-shadow effect. This Hetzer was destroyed by an M10 near Halloville, France, 17 November 1944. Note the 2 periscopes for the driver, one for vision immediately in front of the vehicle and one for longer distance.
61. This American private of K Company, 16th Regiment, 1st Division, poses in front of a Panzer IV/70(V) which he destroyed with a bazooka during a German counterattack near Hamich, Germany, 22 November 1944. The 80mm frontal armour is very evident. Although the front bogies are rubber-tyred, the flange for the gun mantlet tapers to allow for the larger MG port cover on the L/70 version. (US Army Official Photograph)
62. These Panthers were knocked out by men of the 26th Infantry Division in a battle near Gruberling, France, 25 November 1944. The vehicle in the foreground is an Ausf G, with raised engine fans, rain guard over the mantlet, sun visor for the driver's periscopes, and gun-cleaning equipment on the side pannier. The Shermans have bogged down in the soft ground.

62▼

▲63 ▼64

63. Another of Nazi Germany's great engines of war, a Tiger II 'Königstiger', lies impotent in a field near Freialdenhoven, Germany, 28 November 1944, having been holed by a 90mm round from an American M36 tank destroyer. The men are members of the 702nd Tank Destroyer Battalion, 2nd Armored Division, Ninth US Army. One points to the damaged track which stopped the Tiger and set it up for the fatal hit in the turret.
64. Members of the 3rd Armored Division inspect a straw-covered StuG III Ausf G abandoned near Obergeich, Germany, 11 December 1944, no doubt relieved that they did not have to face its powerful cannon and compact hull across the broad fields. This StuG has steel return rollers, but does not appear to have ever been fitted with skirt armour.
65. A Tiger II, formerly of the Heeres schwere Panzerabteilung 506, moves down a street in Gersonsweiler, Germany, having been repaired by the 129th Ordnance Bn, 15 December 1944. The mantlet and roof hatch still bear the inscription, 'Danger, Mined', indicating that the Germans booby-trapped the vehicle before abandoning it. Home-made stars draped on the vehicle identify it as US property now.
66. Members of an anti-tank platoon and their newly-acquired StuG III Ausf G roll down a street near Inden, Germany, 17 December 1944. This StuG carries a thick layer of concrete on the superstructure front and sides, 'Saukopf', waffle-pattern zimmerit, steel return rollers, track chevrons, remote-controlled MG (shown here with an assault rifle in place of the MG) and late-pattern muzzle brake. Numerous wire loops have been spot welded to the hull front and trackguard to secure foliage.

65▼

66▼

▲67

67. A Pz Kpfw IV late Ausf H or early J, captured intact by men of the 101st Airborne Division when it attempted to storm Bastogne, 26 December 1944. This vehicle has the late sprocket/idler, four steel return rollers, interlocked 80mm hull front, schurzen and lots of spare track. Its L/48 cannon with 'H'-pattern muzzle brake has one kill ring and the name 'Lustmolch' painted on it. The vehicle took a hit to the top right front of the turret.

68. This Pz Kpfw IV Ausf J met its end at the hands of an American tank destroyer in Wirtzfeld, Belgium, 17 December 1944, when an anti-tank round smashed through the left side of the turret. The vehicle has the old muffler, late sprocket/idler, steel return rollers, wire mesh schurzen and track chevrons, but lacks zimmerit, vision ports in the turret hatches and super-structure sides and the vertical brackets on the lower rear hull.
▼68

69▲

69. A squad of GIs inspect a thoroughly scorched Panther Ausf G, knocked out at Heiderscheid, Luxembourg, 26 December 1944. One of 450 Panthers available for the Ardennes Offensive, it has the more common, low engine fans and plenty of spare track on the turret.

▲70

▲71 ▼72

70. Two more vehicles from the German spearhead into the Ardennes, knocked out by the 3rd Armored Division during bitter fighting in Hotten, Belgium, 26 December 1944. The Panther Ausf G has the new mantlet, high engine fans and 'ambush' paint scheme. Behind it is a Pz Kpfw IV Ausf J.

71. American soldiers of the 329th Regiment, 83rd Division, calmly stringing communications cable across a Panther Ausf G, knocked out in the battle for Humain, Belgium, 28 December 1944. The vehicle took hits to the bow MG, right front corner of the turret and middle of the mantlet. It has the high engine fans and a small number '80' outlined on the turret side just before a similar-sized German cross.

72. Panther Ausf G with high engine fans, 'chin' mantlet and soft-edge camouflage scheme, knocked out near Buissonville, Belgium, 29 December 1944. This Panther looks relatively new, and has shields around the exhaust pipes. It seems that the driver was slewing the vehicle sharply as the result of track damage when the turret front was fractured by anti-tank rounds.

73. Front ¾ view of a late-production Panzer IV/70(V) produced during Oct–Nov 1944 and disabled during the Ardennes Offensive shortly afterwards. Note the excessive overhang of the barrel, three steel return rollers and steel-tyred bogies in the first two positions.

74. The compact lethality of this Panzer IV/70(V) shows to good effect in this photograph, taken in the Canadian sector. This model lacks zimmerit, and has only three steel return rollers, which places its production at some time after October 1944. (C-84045/Public Archives of Canada)

75. Side view of the same vehicle, which stood less than two metres high. As a remedy to its nose heaviness, caused by the longer gun and 80mm upper hull armour, the first two bogie wheels are of the steel resilient type. The usual schurzen has been pared away leaving only the attachment bolts along the superstructure sides. (C–84044/Public Archives of Canada)

73▲ 74▼
75▼

▲76 ▼77

76. A Pz Kpfw IV Ausf H, disembowelled by determined American resistance near Bastogne, 3 January 1945. This model featured basic 80mm frontal armour, the SSG77 transmission and deletion of side vision ports for the driver and radio operator. Note the muzzle brake and the neat application of zimmerit.
77. The glacis of this knocked out Panther Ausf G is wreathed with evergreens, hiding the partial whitewash job. An American tanker, who helped storm Grandmenil, peers into its blackened turret. This Panther has the high engine fans and visor for the driver's periscope. The hinged hatch for the radio operator lies on the ground in front of the right track.
78. Men of the 67th Armored Regiment, 2nd Armored Division, inspect this Panther Ausf G, abandoned in the woods near Grandmenil, Belgium, after a shell had jammed in the breech of the gun, 4 January 1945. The clean lines of the redesigned hull are shown to good advantage.

78▼

▲79

79. A StuG III Ausf G being towed down Highway 6 in the Mount Lungo area of Italy by a M31 ARV, 13 January 1944. The StuG III has 30mm armour bolted to its front hull and superstructure and is equipped with smoke projectors. The letter 'A' appears on the glacis and the superstructure side.

80. A Tiger II, knocked out near Wardin, Belgium, by gunfire from the 6th Armored Division. The turret side and rear have been penetrated. The rear escape hatch is open and the hatch for the loading port is visible on the roof. Snow obliterates any markings the vehicle may have carried.

81. A rear $\frac{3}{4}$ shot of a partially-whitewashed Tiger II, no. '312', knocked out by the 628th Tank Destroyer Battalion of the 82nd Airborne Division in Belgium, 8 January 1945. Its exhaust stacks seem puny compared to the rest of the vehicle, and would have glowed red hot under operating conditions. The first pair of roadwheels is damaged and the spare track on the turret has been dislodged by a hit which did not penetrate.

82. A 'Wirbelwind' which lost its match with Allied fighter-bombers. This example is based on an up-armoured Pz Kpfw IV Ausf G chassis and was relatively new. Note the rear 'wall' of the shattered turret which afforded room for the FlaK gunner, and how it overhung the turret ring. (Author's collection)

▼80

81▲ 82▼

83. This late-production Panther Ausf G was hit from behind by a tank destroyer moments after holing a Sherman in Sterpigny, Belgium, illustrating the hazards of tanks fighting in built-up areas. Photographed 20 January 1945, this Panther sported the 'chin' mantlet and raised engine fans, and it had the number '412' painted well back on the turret side. (US Army Photograph)

84. Engineers passing a knocked out FlaKpanzer IV on the road to Compogne, Belgium, 15 January 1945. All FlaKpanzers were produced on rebuilt Pz Kpfw IV chassis. This one had steel return rollers, late mufflers and welded plate over the hole for the auxiliary engine muffler. The 2cm FlaKvierling vehicles had nine-sided turrets with the rear 'wall' for the gunner. The elevating armature is visible, as are the flat stowage boxes for extra 2cm barrels over the engine air intakes.

85. Mortar observers from the 358th Infantry Regiment, 90th Infantry Division set up shop in front of a Tiger I Ausf E of the Panzerabteilung (Funklenk) 301, knocked out near Oberwampach, Luxembourg, 21 January 1945. This Tiger was used to control up to three B IV demolition vehicles. The muzzle brake has kept the barrel sleeve from being blown completely off the vehicle.

86. A Flammpanzer 38(t) knocked out in Gros Rederching, France, by the 114th Infantry Regiment, 44th Division, 13 January 1945. Note the longer, sheet-metal false barrel which looks like an ordinary cannon. The bottom of this dummy barrel slotted from the muzzle down to the projector barrel to prevent flaming fuel dripping back on the vehicle. Note the spare track on the superstructure side.

▲83 ▼84

85▲ 86▼

▲87 ▼88

87. Side view of another Flammpanzer 38(t) captured in Oermingen, France and photographed on 23 January 1945. Used first by the 17th SS PzGren Div., these tanks caused great losses for US forces of the 100th Infantry Division and the 2nd French Armoured Division when used around Rimling, France. This vehicle has a vertically-mounted muffler, spoked, 8-hole idler and the number 'S14' stencilled on its side. Note the small, crimped cowling over the flame projector barrel.
88. Front view of the same Flammpanzer 38(t) showing the bulbous gun housing, now occupied by the flame projector and its operator, who viewed his targets through a periscope covered by a sun visor extending through the access port on the top. The shield for the remote-controlled MG in the background makes the visor appear larger than it really is.
89. A whitewashed M3A1 halftrack of the 6th Armored Division passes a shattered Pz Kpfw IV Ausf J most notable for the new swivel hatch for the commander's cupola which replaced the hinged type. Destroyed in the Belgian town of Foy, near Bastogne, in January 1945, this vehicle has wire mesh schurzen, ice grips in its tracks, and the late-pattern muzzle brake.
90. A Tiger II disabled in the Ardennes by a combination of artillery and fighter-bombers. The number '03' is painted over the 'ambush' camouflage scheme. Notice how most of the brackets on the hull side have been stripped away. (US Air Force Photograph)
91. Remarkable shot of a late-war Panther Ausf G disabled near the Siegfried Line in an area strongly attacked by Ninth Air Force fighter-bombers. The number '302' is outlined on the turret side and it has the new mantlet and fan covers. Cowls have been fitted around the exhaust pipes and the jack has been removed from its stowage position on the hull rear. Note that the hatch for the engine deck has been moved, indicating possible engine trouble causing the crew to abandon a brand new Panther. (US Air Force Photograph)

89▲

90▲ 91▼

▲92

▲93

92. A very interesting shot of a Pz Kpfw IV Ausf J with commander's swivel hatch, knocked out in Luxembourg by Ninth Air Force fighter-bombers. These hatches were fitted with a grab handle and pivoted at the three o'clock position. The pipe bracket for the mesh schurzen is clearly shown. The vehicle has the early idler, four steel return rollers and pistol ports in the turret doors. The number '332' appears on the forward turret schurzen along with stencilled man with raised sword on rearing horse insignia. 11 February 1945. (US Air Force Photograph)

93. This snow-covered 'Wirbelwind' was captured in Belgium on 27 January 1945, and was to be sent back to the USA by Third Army Ordnance Int. for further study. One of the 2cm FlaK guns is missing as are all of the flash hiders on the remaining guns. Odd is the fact that a thin-skinned vehicle as high as the 'Wirbelwind' has no winter camouflage applied.

94. One of eighty-six FlaKpanzer IV/2cm Vierlings converted from rebuilt Pz Kpfw IVs, this time an Ausf G with additional 30mm plate bolted to the superstructure front. It has the new sprocket/old idler combination, with rubber return rollers. The hull sides are coated with zimmerit. The flat boxes over the engine air intakes held spare barrels and are open here. Grab handles have been affixed to the turret, which carries the number '031' on its side. Only one barrel has a flash hider. Photographed 9 February 1945 in Hetterschlag, France.

95. Superb rear ¾ view of no. '301', a brand-new, late-production Panther Ausf G, with exhaust flame traps on its muffler, late idler, high engine fans and 'chin' mantlet with rain guard. The mufflers were modified to prevent the torch effect caused by unburnt gases igniting on the hot exhaust pipes which gave away a vehicle's position at night. This vehicle still has the starter crank in place, and evidently ran out of fuel near Clervaux, Luxembourg while retreating. Although mined, the charge failed to explode. This Panther has a soft-edge paint scheme and no zimmerit. (US Air Force Photograph)

94▲ 95▼

▲96 ▼97

98▲

96. US anti-aircraft crewmen swarm over a 'Möbelwagen' destroyed in the town of Hosingen, near the Siegfried Line. The bow MG was not fitted to these particular vehicles, and the superstructure was extended further over the trackguards. Note how the shields have shattered in this instance. The soldier with the carbine examines a German egg grenade. (US Air Force Photograph)
97. A bazookaman from the 142nd Infantry Regiment, 36th Division, looks over a Hetzer which has churned up the streets of Oberhoffen, France, before he knocked it out on 13 February 1945. The bulbous housing for the 7.5cm PaK39 L/48 is fitted with the late-production mantlet. (US Army Official Photograph)
98. Rear view of a late-production Pz Kpfw IV Ausf J with wire mesh schurzen, vertical mufflers, no zimmerit and no vision ports in the turret hatches. The rear of the vehicle has been completely scorched by a fire which reduced the rubber in all the bogies to ash. (National Archives)
99. A soldier examines the cracked turret front of the same vehicle. The wire mesh schurzen was fitted in sections like the plate schurzen, although the former was carried on sections of pipe rather than on angle-iron brackets. (National Archives)

99▼

100. The remains of a Jagdtiger, knocked out by a shell from an M36 tank destroyer, are examined by a soldier of the 776th Tank Destroyer Battalion, 44th Infantry Division, in the Rimling area of France, 28 February 1945. The 250mm armour of the superstructure front shows the cutout for interlocking with the side plates. (US Army Official Photograph)

101. Front ¾ view of a massive Sturmmörser, showing details of its superstructure's interlocked construction. Built on a Tiger I chassis returned for overhaul, this vehicle still carries the original zimmerit on the hull front and lower sides except where special fittings were attached during its conversion. The vision ports for the driver and gunlayer, cut into the 150mm armour, are clearly evident. Note the rifling in the barrel, and vents for escaping gases. The lugs were for attaching counterweights. This Sturmmörser was captured by the 30th Infantry Division on 28 February 1945.

▼100

▼101

102▲ 103▼

102. Top rear view of the same vehicle, showing the escape hatch and demountable crane used to hoist the rockets into the vehicle. The Sturmmörser fired either hollow charge or HE rockets weighing 761lb to a maximum range of 6,179 yards. Extreme sensitivity of the propellant to changes in temperature affected both range and accuracy. At certain angles of impact ricochets could be expected, and on hard ground the projectile could break up. Much, therefore, depended on the slope, undergrowth and nature of the ground.

103. American troops captured this heavily-camouflaged Hetzer near Camp de Bitche, France, 17 March 1945. Black bars were painted on the glacis around the driver's visor in order to confuse enemy gunners. The lugs on the roof for the 2-ton emergency crane, called 'Pilzen' (mushrooms), have been capped, and the remote-controlled MG has been removed from its mount. Note the 'bump' stop on the mantlet flange.

104. Extraordinary side view of a very rare steel-wheeled Panther Ausf G, one of a handful of trial production vehicles that tested the new suspension. A spare roadwheel is carried on the engine deck and track grousers are clustered on the rear of the hull side. Spare track links obscure the number '221' on the turret which has the old mantlet. Every hatch is open, including the one on the engine deck, and the ground around the tank is littered with empty jerrycans, indicating that the crew was forced to leave a vehicle immobilized by mechanical trouble.

▲105

▲106

▲107

105. The penultimate Pz Kpfw IV Ausf J, its towing brackets formed from the extended hull sides, but still with four steel return rollers. Its 80mm front superstructure armour is clearly visible as is its bullet-riddled wire mesh schurzen. There are no pistol ports in the turret doors and the cannon is minus its muzzle brake. Quite possibly this vehicle had a commander's swivel hatch as well. Photographed in Luxembourg in 1945. (US Air Force Photograph)
106. A Jagdpanther and an American M36 tank destroyer stand where they were knocked out in a field near Kaimig, Germany, 17 March 1945, mute evidence of the see-saw nature of attack and counterattack. The level ground and open spaces were ideal conditions for these tank destroyers' long-range, hard-hitting cannon. The Jagdpanther, no. '123', has the late-war idlers and the tube for the gun-cleaning tools across the engine deck. Note the large stowage box fitted on the rear of the superstructure.
107. No. '314' belonged to Panzerjägerabteilung 653, and was one of the small number of Jagdtigers built with the Porsche-designed longitudinal torsion bar suspension plus the old drive sprocket. This vehicle lost all its trackguards and managed to hang itself up on a small slope beside a road. Note the 'ambush' paint scheme.
108. These two Panzer IV/70(V)s were abandoned in the face of US First Army troops outside Oberpleis, Germany, 25 March 1945. Unusual is the fact that both have all rubber-tyred bogies, but only three steel return rollers. The vehicle in the foreground has vertical mufflers, three kill rings on the barrel and the number '201' painted over the 'ambush' paint scheme.

◀108

09. Excellent side view of 'anzer IV/70(A) knocked out y the 78th Division in Jekerath, Germany, 28 March 945. This vehicle was roduced after December 944, and was based on the late 'z Kpfw IV Ausf J chassis, vith the hull sides extended nd drilled to form tow hackles. There are only three teel return rollers and the first our bogie wheels are steel-yred. A round passing through he nearly transparent mesh churzen and into the engine ompartment stopped this 'ehicle.

10. Near Marienburg, Germany, 28 March 1945, a rd Armored Division M4A1, ts cast hull reinforced with louble slabs of sheet armour, olls past a Pz Kpfw IV with xtra 30mm armour bolted to he superstructure front and 0mm plate welded to the hull ront, demonstrating how the German vehicle's lower rmour could be beefed up nore completely with less veight than its higher American counterpart. The panzer has a vision port for the driver and is an early Ausf H or ate G depending on the drive sprockets.

111. This tank remanufacturing plant in Magdeburg, Germany, belonged to Krupp, and even though heavily bombed in August 1944, the assembly section remained active until five months before its capture in April 1945. Outside are five Pz Kpfw III Ausf Gs, all lacking their main armament. The one in the foreground has the early idler/tailplate with late sprocket, cupola and 40cm track. The others have all been brought up to 'L' standards with up-armoured tailplate and spaced mantlet armour although some still have the old cupola and 36cm track! 20 April 1945.

112. War booty. At the head of the line is a late model Jagdpanther mounting the two-piece 8.8cm PaK43/4 and having the rather uncharacteristic number '59' on its side. The heavier bolt-on collar and the driver's single episcope are traits of a late-production vehicle. Next in line are three 'Wirbelwinds', the muzzles of all their guns covered. The pointed bows and long barrels of three Panzer IV/70(V)s are just visible at the end of the row. (PA–52479/ Public Archives of Canada)

▲113

▲114 ▼115

113. A Sherman tank the 750th Tank Battalion is credited with destroying this Jagdtiger of the schwe Panzerabteilung 512, seen here in the woods of Offensen, Germany, 9 April 1945, after losing a track and sliding off the road. Note how the travel lock folds down over th headlamp, and the twi grab handles necessary to lift the swivel hatche for the driver and radic operator. The three 'Pilzen' for the emergency crane were welded to the front, sid and rear tops of the superstructure.

114. Civilians in the town of Osterode, Germany silently watcl a GI inspect a Tiger II which was knocked out by a 90mm round burning through the side of its turret. The Tiger is painted in the 'ambush' scheme and all the hatches are open Notice how far the tracks extend past the hull sides and how the front slope of the turret roof gave the commander decent forward observation. A 88mm round is proppec against the turret, testimony to the once formidable offensive power of this vehicle. 12 April 1945.

115. A Sturmmörser captured in the outskirts of Drolshagen, Germany by 8th Division infantrymen on 11 April 1945. These vehicles were designed to give close support to infantry in the assault on strongly defended localities, and this one was beefed up with additional armour bolted on the hull front. Note the massive counterweight, different brackets on the superstructure side and the absence of zimmerit. The crane, ventilator and 'Nahverteidigungs-waffe' on the roof are all visible.

116. Front ¾ view of a burned-out Panther Ausf G having the steel-wheeled suspension fitted. Note the condition of the rear portion of the suspension and how far the radio operator's hatch swung open.
117. Crew members ride exposed on a line of Sturmgeschütz IVs moving into Ivea, Italy, to surrender to the US 34th Division on 5 May 1945. These vehicles have home-made travel locks, concrete on the right front superstructure and extra sloping armour plate fitted in front of the drivers' compartments. A Bergepanzer III brings up the rear.
118. The redesigned track of this late-production Jagdtiger lies piled up where it was shed, allowing a view of the modified drive sprocket. In order to fit the new track, every other tooth of the old sprocket was cut off with a torch. The glacis and mantlet were heavily gouged by shellfire as it attempted to hold a strategic position overlooking a valley in the Harz Mountains near St Adreasberg, Germany, 16 April 1945.

116▲

117▲ 118▼

▲119

120▲

121▲

119. An interrogation officer with the 69th Infantry Division poses atop a 15cm schwere Panzerhaubitze Pz Kpfw III/IV 'Hummel' which he captured single-handed near Wurzen, Germany, 25 April 1945. This vehicle has the standard three-colour camouflage scheme and the driver's full-width compartment introduced from early 1944. The aiming spikes on the glacis presumably enabled the driver to align the 'Hummel'.
120. At the same vehicle park are these two vehicles: a Bergepanther built on the Ausf D chassis and a 'Möbelwagen' minus its gun and drop side armour. The Bergepanther carries a very thick application of zimmerit and has a carrying bracket welded to its glacis for its pulley. Quite possibly it was used in this position as well. The 'Möbelwagen' has the late-drive sprocket, steel return rollers and interlocked hull armour. Note the hinges for the shields on the corners of the superstructure, and the 'cage' on the gun mount. The mount itself fitted directly on top of the new superstucture roof and is elevated to 90°. All the vehicles in this park had shipping instructions on black rectangles painted on them. (G.B. Jarrett collection, via Bill Miley)
121. Front ¾ view of a Pz Kpfw III Ausf N in a vehicle park at the end of hostilities. Note the spaced armour across the superstructure front and the serial number on the driver's visor. The short 7.5cm gun was still effective against armour when firing hollow charge rounds and this final version of the Pz Kpfw III series was well liked by its crews. (G.B. Jarrett collection, via Bill Miley)
122. An interesting collection of AFVs surrendered to the Canadians. In the foreground are two StuG III Ausf Gs with spoked steel return rollers, remote-controlled MGs, coaxial MGs in the mantlet, travel locks, late-pattern muzzle brakes and no zimmerit. Both have a good share of kill rings and both carry women's names on their hulls. Next to them is a StuG III Ausf D, retroactively fitted with an MG shield for the gunner. Behind them is a Pz Kpfw III Ausf N. (PA–52083/Public Archives of Canada)

122▼

▲123 ▼124

123. German crews turn over their tanks outside Oslo, Norway, 10 June 1945. Most of the tanks are Pz Kpfw III Ausf Ns with zimmerit, schurzen and bolt-on armour, but there are several Ausf Js as well. Note the smoke bomb dischargers on the turret sides of the vehicle in the foreground, and how all the muzzles have been capped.
124. A fitting photograph for the end of this book and the end of the Panzers. An American and a Russian soldier pose atop the heaviest and most powerful vehicle of the Panzertruppen, during the link-up of the two armies. One of the last to see action, it carries the only unit insignia ever seen on a Jagdtiger – a toy bear . . . (Author's collection)